# The
# Official Rules of
# Soccer

CHICAGO

Cover photo: J. Brett Whitesell, RB Sports Photography
Typography: Marilyn Justman

This book is available in quantity at special discounts for your group or organi-
zation. For further information contact:

Triumph books
644 South Clark Street, Suite 2000
Chicago, IL 60605
312/ 939-3330
Fax: 312/ 663-3557

PRINTED IN CANADA

# User's Guide

This edition of the Official Laws of the Game has been designed to give soccer fans of all ages a quick and easy reference guide to the action on the field.

Diagrams illustrating off-side points, instructions on taking kicks from the penalty-marks, and signals by the referee and linesmen can all be found here following the Laws themselves.

Any amendments to Laws and Decisions since the last edition of these Laws are indicated by a <u>double underline</u>.

Please note that these rules are subject to the agreement of the National Associations as specified on the Notes page.

# Table of Contents

## Notes

Subject to the agreement of the National Association concerned and provided the principles of these Laws are maintained, the Laws may be modified in their application for matches for players of under 16 years of age, for women's football and for veterans' football (over 35 years).

Any or all of the following modifications are permissible:

- (a) size of the field of play;
- (b) size, weight and material of the ball;
- (c) width between the goalposts and height of the cross-bar from the ground;
- (d) the duration of the periods of play;
- (e) number of substitutions.

Further modifications are only possible with the consent of the International Football Association Board.

References to the male gender within the Laws of the Game in respect of referees, linesmen, players or officials are for simplification and refer to both males and females.

# The Field of Play

# The Field of Play

The field of play and appurtenances shall be as shown in the following plan:

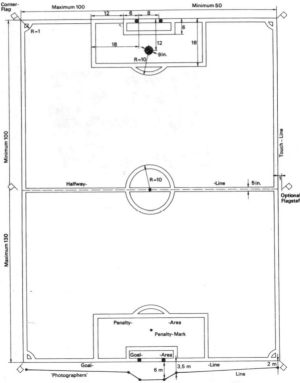

*(N. B. All measurements are in yards and inches unless otherwise marked )*

# LAW I **The Field of Play**

(1) **Dimensions.** The field of play shall be rectangular, its length being not more than 130 yards nor less than 100 yards and its breadth not more than 100 yards nor less than 50 yards. (In international matches the length shall be not more than 120 yards nor less than 110 yards and the breadth not more than 80 yards nor less than 70 yards.) The length shall in all cases exceed the breadth.

(2) **Marking.** The field of play shall be marked with distinctive lines, not more than 5 inches in width (not by a V-shaped rut) in accordance with the plan, the longer boundary lines being called the touch-lines and the shorter the goal-lines. A flag on a post not less than 5 ft. high and having a non-pointed top, shall be placed at each corner; a similar flag-post may be placed opposite the half-way line on each side of the field of play, not less than 1 yard outside the touch-line.

A halfway-line shall be marked out across the field of play. The centre of the field of play shall be indicated by a suitable mark and a circle with a 10-yards radius shall be marked round it.

(3) **The Goal-Area.** At each end of the field of play two lines shall be drawn at right-angles to the goal-line, 6 yards from each goal-post. These shall extend into the field of play for a distance of 6 yards and shall be joined by a line drawn parallel with the goal-line. Each of the spaces enclosed by these lines and the goal-line shall be called a goal-area.

(4) **The Penalty-Area.** At each end of the field of play two lines shall be drawn at right-angles to the goal-line, 18 yards from each goal-post. These shall extend into the field of play for a distance of 18 yards and shall be joined by a line drawn parallel with the goal-line. Each of the spaces enclosed by these lines and the goal-line shall be called a penalty-area. A suitable mark shall be made within each penalty-area, 12 yards from the mid-point of the goal-line, measured along an undrawn line at right-angles thereto. These shall be the penalty-kick marks. From each

penalty-kick mark an arc of a circle, having a radius of 10 yards, shall be drawn outside the penalty-area.

(5) **The Corner-Area.** From each corner-flag post a quarter circle, having a radius of 1 yard, shall be drawn inside the field of play.

(6) **The Goals.** The goals shall be placed on the centre of each goal-line and shall consist of two upright posts, equidistant from the corner flags and 8 yards apart (inside measurement), joined by a horizontal crossbar, the lower edge of which shall be 8 ft. from the ground.

<u>For safety reasons, the goals, including those which are portable, must be anchored securely to the ground.</u>

The width and depth of the cross-bars shall not exceed 5 inches (12 cm). The goal-posts and the cross-bars shall have the same width.

Nets[1] may be attached to the posts,

---

[1] **Goal nets.** The use of nets made of hemp, jute or nylon is permitted. The nylon strings may, however, not be thinner than those made of hemp or jute.

cross-bars and ground behind the goals.
They should be appropriately
supported and be so placed as to allow
the goal-keeper ample room.

## LAW I Decisions of the International F.A. Board

(1) In international matches the dimensions of the
field of play shall be: maximum 110 x 75
metres; minimum 100 x 64 metres.

(2) National Associations must adhere strictly to
these dimensions. Each National Association
organising an international match must advise
the visiting Association, before the match, of
the place and the dimensions of the field of play.

(3) The Board has approved this table of
measurements for the Laws of the Game:

| | |
|---|---|
| 130 yards | 120 Metres |
| 120 yards | 110 |
| 110 yards | 100 |
| 100 yards | 90 |
| 80 yards | 75 |
| 70 yards | 64 |
| 50 yards | 45 |
| 18 yards | 16.50 |
| 12 yards | 11 |
| 10 yards | 9.15 |
| 8 yards | 7.32 |
| 6 yards | 5.50 |
| 1 Yard | 1 |
| 8 feet | 2.44 |
| 5 feet | 1.50 |

28 inches......0.71
27 inches......0.68
9 inches......0.22
5 inches......0.12
3/4 inch......0.019
1/2 inch......0.0127
3/8 inch......0.010
14 ounces......396 grams
16 ounces......453 grams
8.5 lb/sq.in.......600 gr/cm$^2$
15.6 lb/sq.in.......1100 gr/cm$^2$

(4) The goal-line shall be marked the same width as the depth of the goal-posts and the cross-bar, so that the goal-line and goal-posts will conform to the same interior and exterior edges.

(5) The 6 yards (for the outline of the goal-area) and the 18 yards (for the outline of the penalty-area) which have to be measured along the goal-line, must start from the inner sides of the goal-posts.

(6) The space within the inside areas of the field of play includes the width of the lines marking these areas.

(7) All Associations shall provide standard equipment, particularly in international matches, when the Laws of the Game must be complied with in every respect and especially with regard to the size of the ball and other equipment which must conform to the regulations. All cases of failure to provide standard equipment must be reported to FIFA.

(8) In a match played under the rules of a competition if the cross-bar becomes displaced or broken, play shall be stopped and the match abandoned unless the cross-bar has been repaired and replaced in position or a new one provided without such being a danger to the players. A rope is not considered to be a satisfactory substitute for a cross-bar.

In a friendly match, by mutual consent, play may be resumed without the cross-bar provided it has been removed and no longer constitutes a danger to the players. In these circumstances, a rope may be used as a substitute for a cross-bar. If a rope is not used and the ball crosses the goal-line at a point which, in the opinion of the referee is below where the cross-bar should have been, he shall award a goal.

The game shall be restarted by the referee dropping the ball at the place where it was when play was stopped, unless it was within the goal-area at that time, in which case it shall be dropped on that part of the goal-area line which runs parallel to the goal-line, at the point where the ball was when play was stopped.

(9) National Associations may specify such maximum and minimum dimensions for the cross-bars and goal-posts, within the limits laid down in Law I, as they consider appropriate.

(10) Goal-posts and cross-bars must be made of wood, metal or other approved material as decided from time to time by the International

F.A. Board. They may be square, rectangular, round, half-round or elliptical in shape.

Goal-posts and cross-bars made of other materials and in other shapes are not permitted. The goal-posts must be of white colour.

(11) 'Curtain-raisers' to international matches should only be played following agreement on the day of the match, and taking into account the condition of the field of play, between representatives of the two Associations and the referee (of the international match).

(12) National Associations, particularly in international matches, should

— restrict the number of photographers around the field of play,

— have a line (photographers' line) marked behind the goal-lines at least two metres from the corner flag going through a point situated at least 3.5 metres behind the intersection of the goal-line with the line marking the goal-area to a point situated at least six metres behind the goal-posts,

— prohibit photographers from passing over these lines,

— forbid the use of artificial lighting in the form of "flashlights".

# The Ball

# LAW II **The Ball**

The ball shall be spherical; the outer casing shall be of leather or other approved materials. No material shall be used in its construction which might prove dangerous to the players.

The circumference of the ball shall not be more than 28 in. and not less than 27 in. The weight of the ball at the start of the game shall not be more than 16 oz. nor less than 14 oz. The pressure shall be equal to 0.6-1.1 atmosphere (=600-1,100 gr/cm$^2$) at sea level. The ball shall not be changed during the game unless authorized by the referee.

## LAW II **Decisions of the International F.A. Board**

(1) The ball used in any match shall be considered the property of the Association or Club on whose ground the match is played, and at the close of play it must be returned to the referee.

(2) The International Board, from time to time, shall decide what constitutes approved materials. Any approved material shall be certified as such by the International Board.

(3) The Board has approved these equivalents of the weights specified in the Law: 14 to 16 ounces = 396 to 453 grammes.

(4) If the ball bursts or becomes deflated during the course of a match, the game shall be stopped and restarted by dropping the new ball at the place where the first ball became defective, unless it was within the goal-area at that time, in which case it shall be dropped on that part of the goal-area line which runs parallel to the goal-line, at the point nearest to where the ball was when play was stopped.

(5) If this happens during a stoppage of the game (place-kick, goal-kick, corner-kick, free-kick, penalty-kick or throw-in), the game shall be restarted accordingly.

# Number of Players

# LAW III **Number of Players**

(1) A match shall be played by two teams, each consisting of not more than eleven players, one of whom shall be the goalkeeper.

(2) Substitutes may be used in any match played under the rules of an official competition under the jurisdiction of FIFA, Confederations or National Associations, subject to the following conditions:

(a) that the authority of the international association(s) or National Association(s) concerned has been obtained.

(b) that, subject to the restriction contained in the following paragraphs (c) <u>and (d)</u>, the rules of a competition shall state how many, if any, substitutes may be <u>designated</u> and how many of those <u>designated</u> may be used.

(c) that a team shall not be permitted to use more than two substitutes in any match who must be chosen from not more than five players whose names may (subject to the rules of the competition) be required to be given to the referee prior to the commencement of the match.

(d) <u>Notwithstanding the limitation imposed in (c), a team may also use a third substitute provided that he is designated as a substitute goalkeeper, who may be used to replace only the goalkeeper.</u>

<u>If, however, the goalkeeper is ordered off, the designated substitute goalkeeper may subsequently replace another player of the same team and play as goalkeeper.</u>

(3) Substitutes may be used in any other match, provided that the two teams concerned reach agreement on a maximum number, not exceeding five, and that the terms of such agreement are intimated to the referee, before the match. If the referee is not informed, or if the teams fail to reach agreement, no more than two substitutes shall be permitted. In all cases the substitutes

must be chosen from not more than five players whose names may be required to be given to the referee prior to the commencement of the match.

(4) Any of the other players may change places with the goalkeeper, provided that the referee is informed before the change is made, and provided also that the change is made during a stoppage of the game.

(5) When a goalkeeper or any other player is to be replaced by a substitute, the following conditions shall be observed:

(a) The referee shall be informed of the proposed substitution, before it is made.

(b) The substitute shall not enter the field of play until the player he is replacing has left, and then only after having received a signal from the referee.

(c) He shall enter the field during a stoppage in the game, and at the halfway line.

(d) A player who has been replaced shall not take any further part in the game.

(e) A substitute shall be subject to the authority and jurisdiction of the referee whether called upon to play or not.

(f) The substitution is completed when the substitute enters the field of play, from which moment he becomes a player and the player whom he is replacing ceases to be a player.

### Punishment:

(a) Play shall not be stopped for an infringement of paragraph 4. The players concerned shall be cautioned immediately the ball goes out of play.

(b) If a substitute enters the field of play without the authority of the referee, play shall be stopped. The substitute shall be cautioned and removed from the field or sent off according to the circumstances. The game shall be restarted by the referee dropping the ball at the

place where it was when play was
stopped, unless it was within the
goal-area at that time, in which
case it shall be dropped on that
part of the goal-area line which
runs parallel to the goal-line, at the
point nearest to where the ball was
when play was stopped.

(c) For any other infringement of this
Law, the player concerned shall be
cautioned, and if the game is
stopped by the referee to
administer the caution, it shall be
restarted by an indirect free-kick, to
be taken by a player of the
opposing team from the place
where the ball was when play was
stopped, subject to the overriding
conditions imposed in Law XIII.

(d) If a competition's rules require the
names of substitutes to be given to
the referee prior to the
commencement of the match,
then failure to do so will mean that
no substitutes can be permitted.

# LAW III Decisions of the International F.A. Board

(1) The minimum number of players in a team is left to the discretion of National Associations.

(2) The Board is of the opinion that a match should not be considered valid if there are fewer than seven players in either of the teams.

(3) A player who has been ordered off before play begins may only be replaced by one of the named substitutes. The kick-off must not be delayed to allow the substitute to join his team.

A player who has been ordered off after play has started may not be replaced.

A named substitute who has been ordered off, either before or after play has started, may not be replaced.

(This decision only relates to players who are ordered off under Law XII. It does not apply to players who have infringed Law IV.)

# Players'
# Equipment

# LAW IV **Players' Equipment**

(1) (a) The basic compulsory equipment of a player shall consist of a jersey or shirt, shorts, stockings, shinguards and footwear.

(b) A player shall not wear anything which is dangerous to another player.

(2) Shinguards, which must be covered entirely by the stockings, shall be made of a suitable material (rubber, plastic, polyurethane or similar substance) and shall afford a reasonable degree of protection.

(3) The goalkeeper shall wear colours which distinguish him from the other players and from the referee.

**Punishment:**

> For any infringement of this Law, the player at fault shall be instructed to leave the field of play by the referee, to adjust his equipment or obtain any missing equipment, when the ball next ceases to be in play, unless by then the player has already corrected his equip-

ment. Play shall not be stopped immediately for an infringement of this Law. A player who is instructed to leave the field to adjust his equipment or obtain missing equipment shall not return without first reporting to the referee, who shall satisfy himself that the player's equipment is in order. The player shall only re-enter the game at a moment when the ball has ceased to be in play.

## LAW IV Decisions of the International F.A. Board

(1) In international matches, international competitions, international club competitions and friendly matches between clubs of different National Associations, the referee, prior to the start of the game, shall inspect the players' equipment and prevent any player whose equipment does not conform to the requirements of this Law from playing until such time as it does comply. The rules of any competition may include a similar provision.

(2) If the referee finds that a player is wearing articles not permitted by the Laws and which may constitute a danger to other players, he shall order him to take them off. If he fails to carry out the referee's instruction, the player shall not take part in the match.

(3)  A player who has been prevented from taking part in the game or a player who has been sent off the field for infringing Law IV must report to the referee during a stoppage of the game and may not enter or re-enter the field of play unless and until the referee has satisfied himself that the player is no longer infringing Law IV.

(4)  A player who has been prevented from taking part in a game or who has been sent off because of an infringement of Law IV, and who enters or re-enters the field of play to join or re-join his team, in breach of the conditions of Law XII, (j), shall be cautioned.

If the referee stops the game to administer the caution, the game shall be restarted by an indirect free-kick, taken by a player of the opposing side, from the place where the ball was when the referee stopped the game, subject to the overriding conditions imposed in Law XIII.

# Referees

# LAW V **Referees**

A referee shall be appointed to officiate in each game. His authority and the exercise of the powers granted to him by the Laws of the Game commence as soon as he enters the field of play.

His power of penalising shall extend to offences committed when play has been temporarily suspended, or when the ball is out of play. His decision on points of fact connected with the play shall be final, so far as the result of the game is concerned. He shall:

(a) enforce the Laws.

(b) refrain from penalising in cases where he is satisfied that, by doing so, he would be giving an advantage to the offending team.

(c) keep a record of the game; act as timekeeper and allow the full or agreed time, adding thereto all time lost through accident or other cause,

**(d)** have discretionary power to stop the game for any infringement of the Laws and to suspend or terminate the game whenever, by reason of the elements, interference by spectators, or other cause, he deems such stoppage necessary. In such case he shall submit a detailed report to the competent authority, within the stipulated time, and in accordance with the provisions set up by the National Association under whose jurisdiction the match was played. Reports will be deemed to be made when received in the ordinary course of post.

**(e)** from the time he enters the field of play, caution and show a yellow card to any player guilty of misconduct or ungentlemanly behaviour. In such cases the referee shall send the name of the offender to the competent authority, within the stipulated time, and in accordance with the provisions set up by the National Association under whose jurisdiction the match was played.

(f) allow no person other than the players and linesmen to enter the field of play without his permission.

(g) stop the game if, in his opinion, a player has been seriously injured; have the player removed as soon as possible from the field of play, and immediately resume the game. If a player is slightly injured, the game shall not be stopped until the ball has ceased to be in play. A player who is able to go to the touch-or goal-line for attention of any kind, shall not be treated on the field of play.

(h) send off the field of play and show a red card to any player who, in his opinion, is guilty of violent conduct, serious foul play, the use of foul or abusive language or who persists in misconduct after having received a caution.

(i) signal for recommencement of the game after all stoppages.

(j) decide that the ball provided for a match meets with the requirements of Law II.

# LAW V Decisions of the International F.A. Board

(1) Referees in international matches shall wear a blazer or blouse the colour of which is distinct from the colours worn by the contesting teams.

(2) Referees for international matches will be selected from a neutral country unless the countries concerned agree to appoint their own officials.

(3) The referee must be chosen from the official List of International Referees. This need not apply to amateur and youth international matches.

(4) The referee shall report to the appropriate authority misconduct or any misdemeanour on the part of spectators, officials, players, named substitutes or other persons which take place either on the field of play or in its vicinity at any time prior to, during, or after the match in question so that appropriate action can be taken by the authority concerned.

(5) Linesmen are assistants of the referee. In no case shall the referee consider the intervention of a linesman if he himself has seen the incident and from his position on the field, is better able to judge. With this reserve, and the linesman neutral, the referee can consider the intervention, and if the information of the linesman applies to that phase of the game

immediately before the scoring of a goal, the
referee may act thereon and cancel the goal.

(6) The referee, however, can only reverse his first
decision so long as the game has not been
restarted.

(7) If the referee has decided to apply the
advantage clause and to let the game proceed,
he cannot revoke his decision if the presumed
advantage has not been realised, even though he
has not, by any gesture, indicated his decision.
This does not exempt the offending player
from being dealt with by the referee.

(8) The Laws of the Game are intended to provide
that the games should be played with as little
interference as possible, and in this view it is
the duty of referees to penalise only deliberate
breaches of the Law. Constant whistling for
trifling and doubtful breaches produces bad
feeling and loss of temper on the part of the
players and spoils the pleasure of spectators.

(9) By par. (d) of Law V the referee is empowered
to terminate a match in the event of grave
disorder, but he has no power or right to
decide, in such event, that either team is
disqualified and thereby the loser of the match.
He must send a detailed report to the proper
authority who alone has power to deal further
with this matter.

(10) If a player commits two infringements of a
different nature at the same time, the referee
shall punish the more serious offence.

(11) It is the duty of the referee to act upon the information of neutral linesmen with regard to incidents that do not come under the personal notice of the referee.

(12) The referee shall not allow any person to enter the field of play until play has stopped, and only then if he has given him a signal to do so.

**(13) The coach may convey tactical instructions to players during the match. The coach and other officials, however, must remain within the confines of the technical area\* where such an area is provided and they must conduct themselves, at all times, in a responsible manner.**

**(14) In tournaments or competitions where a fourth official is appointed, his role and duties shall be in accordance with the guide-lines approved by the International Football Association Board.**

---

\*For top-level football, the technical area may be defined in terms of the length of the bench plus one metre at each side of the bench, and the area in front of the bench up to one metre parallel to the touch-line.

# Linesmen

## LAW VI **Linesmen**

Two linesmen shall be appointed, whose duty (subject to the decision of the referee) shall be to indicate:

(a) when the ball is out of play,

(b) which side is entitled to a corner-kick, goal-kick or throw-in,

(c) when a substitution is desired.

They shall also assist the referee to control the game in accordance with the Laws. In the event of undue interference or improper conduct by a linesman, the referee shall dispense with his services and arrange for a substitute to be appointed. (The matter shall be reported by the referee to the competent authority.) The linesmen should be equipped with flags by the club on whose ground the match is played.

## LAW VI  Decisions of the International F.A. Board

(1) Linesmen, where neutral, shall draw the referee's attention to any breach of the Laws of the Game of which they become aware if they consider that the referee may not have seen it, but the referee shall always be the judge of the decision to be taken.

(2) National Associations are advised to appoint official referees of neutral nationality to act as linesmen in international matches.

(3) In international matches linesmen's flags shall be of a vivid colour, bright reds and yellows. Such flags are recommended for use in all other matches.

(4) A linesman may be subject to disciplinary action only upon a report of the referee for unjustified interference or insufficient assistance.

# Duration of the Game

# LAW VII **Duration of the Game**

The duration of the game shall be two equal periods of 45 minutes, unless otherwise mutually agreed upon, subject to the following:

(a) Allowance shall be made in either period for all time lost through substitution, the transport from the field of injured players, time-wasting or other cause, the amount of which shall be a matter for the discretion of the referee.

(b) Time shall be extended to permit penalty-kick being taken at or after the expiration of the normal period in either half.

At half-time the interval shall not exceed five minutes except by consent of the referee.

## LAW VII **Decisions of the International F.A. Board**

(1) If a match has been stopped by the referee, before the completion of the time specified in the rules, for any reason stated in Law V, it must be replayed in full unless the rules of the

competition concerned provide for the result of the match at the time of such stoppage to stand.

(2) Players have a right to an interval at half-time.

# The Start of Play

## LAW VIII **The Start of Play**

(a) **At the beginning of the game**, choice of ends and the kick-off shall be decided by the toss of a coin. The team winning the toss shall have the option of choice of ends or the kick-off. The referee having given a signal, the game shall be started by a player taking a place-kick (i.e. a kick at the ball while it is stationary on the ground in the centre of the field of play) into his opponents' half of the field of play. Every player shall be in his own half of the field and every player of the team opposing that of the kicker shall remain not less than 10 yards from the ball until it is kicked-off; it shall not be deemed in play until it has travelled the distance of its own circumference. The kicker shall not play the ball a second time until it has been touched or played by another player.

(b) **After a goal has been scored**, the game shall be restarted in like manner by a player of the team losing the goal.

(c) **After half-time;** when restarting after half-time, ends shall be changed and the kick-off shall be taken by a player of the opposite team to that of the player who started the game.

**Punishment:**

For any infringement of this Law, the kick-off shall be retaken, except in the case of the kicker playing the ball again before it has been touched or played by another player; for this offence an indirect free-kick shall be taken by a player of the opposing team from the place where the infringement occurred, subject to the overriding conditions imposed in Law XIII.

A goal shall not be scored direct from a kick-off.

(d) **After any other temporary suspension;** when restarting the game after a temporary suspension of play from any cause not mentioned elsewhere in these Laws, provided that immediately prior to the suspension the ball has not passed over the touch- or goal-lines, the referee shall drop the ball at the place where it was when play was suspended, unless it was within the goal-area at that time, in which case it shall be dropped on that part of the goal-area line which runs parallel to the goal-line, at the point nearest to where the ball was when play was stopped. It shall be deemed in play when it has touched the ground; if, however, it goes over the touch- or goal-lines after it has been dropped by the referee, but before it is touched by a player, the referee shall again drop it. A player shall not play the ball until it has touched the ground. If this section of the Laws is not complied with the referee shall again drop the ball.

## LAW VIII Decisions of the International F.A. Board

(1) If, when the referee drops the ball, a player infringes any of the Laws before the ball has touched the ground, the player concerned shall be cautioned or sent off the field according to the seriousness of the offence, but a free-kick cannot be awarded to the opposing team because the ball was not in play at the time of the offence. The ball shall therefore be again dropped by the referee.

(2) Kicking-off by persons other than the players competing in a match is prohibited.

# Ball In and Out of Play

# LAW IX **Ball In and Out of Play**

The ball is out of play:

(a) when it has wholly crossed the goal-line or touch-line, whether on the ground or in the air.

(b) when the game has been stopped by the referee.

The ball is in play at all other times from the start of the match to the finish including:

(a) if it rebounds from a goal-post, cross-bar or corner-flag post into the field of play.

(b) if it rebounds off either the referee or linesmen when they are in the field of play.

(c) in the event of a supposed infringement of Laws, until a decision is given.

## LAW IX Decisions of the International F.A. Board

(1) The lines belong to the areas of which they are the boundaries. In consequence, the touch-lines and the goal-lines belong to the field of play.

# Method of Scoring

# LAW X **Method of Scoring**

Except as otherwise provided by these Laws, a goal is scored when the whole of the ball has passed over the goal-line, between the goal-posts and under the cross-bar, provided it has not been thrown, carried or intentionally propelled by hand or arm, by a player of the attacking side, except in the case of a goalkeeper, who is within his own penalty-area.

The team scoring the greater number of goals during a game shall be the winner; if no goals or an equal number of goals are scored, the game shall be termed a "draw".

## LAW X **Decisions of the International F.A. Board**

(1) Law X defines the only method according to which a match is won or drawn; no variation whatsoever can be authorised.

(2) A goal cannot in any case be allowed if the ball has been prevented by some outside agent from passing over the goal-line. If this happens in the normal course of play, other than at the taking of a penalty-kick: the game must be stopped

and restarted by the referee dropping the ball at the place where the ball came into contact with the interference, unless it was within the goal-area at that time, in which case it shall be dropped on that part of the goal-area line which runs parallel to the goal line, at the point nearest to where the ball was when play was stopped.

(3) If, when the ball is going into goal, a spectator enters the field before it passes wholly over the goal-line and tries to prevent a score, a goal shall be allowed if the ball goes into goal unless the spectator has made contact with the ball or has interfered with play, in which case the referee shall stop the game and restart it by dropping the ball at the place where the contact or interference occurred, unless it was within the goal-area at that time, in which case it shall be dropped on the part of the goal-area line which runs parallel to the goal-line, at the point nearest to where the ball was when play was stopped.

# Off-Side

# LAW XI **Off-side**

1. A player is in an off-side position if he is nearer to his opponents' goal-line than the ball, unless:

   (a) he is in his own half of the field of play, or

   (b) he is not nearer to his opponents' goal-line than at least two of his opponents.

2. A player shall only be declared offside and penalised for being in an offside position, if, at the moment the ball touches, or is played by, one of his team, he is, in the opinion of the referee

   (a) interfering with play or with an opponent, or

   (b) seeking to gain an advantage by being in that position.

3. A player shall not be declared offside by the referee

   (a) merely because of his being in an off-side position, or

   **(b)** if he receives the ball direct from a
   goal-kick, a corner-kick or a
   throw-in.

4. If a player is declared offside, the
   referee shall award an indirect
   free-kick, which shall be taken by a
   player of the opposing team from
   where the infringement occurred,
   unless the offence is committed by a
   player in his opponents' goal area, in
   which case the free-kick shall be taken
   from any point within the goal area.

## LAW XI Decisions of the International F.A. Board

(1) Off-side shall not be judged at the moment the
    player in question receives the ball, but at the
    moment when the ball is passed to him by one
    of his own side. A player who is not in an
    off-side position when one of his colleagues
    passes the ball to him or takes a free-kick, does
    not therefore become off-side if he goes forward
    during the flight of the ball.

(2) A player who is level with the second last
    opponent or with the last two opponents is not
    in an off-side position.

# Fouls and
# Misconduct

# LAW XII **Fouls and Misconduct**

A player who intentionally commits any of the following nine offences:

DIRECT

(a) kicks or attempts to kick an opponent;

(b) trips an opponent, i.e. throwing or attempting to throw him by the use of the legs, or by stooping in front of or behind him;

(c) jumps at an opponent;

(d) charges an opponent in a violent or dangerous manner;

(e) charges an opponent from behind unless the latter is obstructing;

(f) strikes or attempts to strike an opponent or spits at him;

(g) holds an opponent;

(h) pushes an opponent;

(i) handles the ball, i.e. carries, strikes, or propels the ball with his hand or arm; (this does not apply to the goalkeeper within his own penalty area);

shall be penalised by the award of a direct free-kick to be taken by the opposing team from the place where the offence occurred, unless the offence is committed by a player in his opponents' goal area, in which case the free-kick shall be taken from any point within the goal area.

Should a player of the defending team intentionally commit one of the above nine offences within the penalty area, he shall be penalised by a penalty-kick.

A penalty-kick can be awarded irrespective of the position of the ball, if in play, at the time of offence within the penalty area is committed.

A player committing any of the five following offences:

1.  playing in a manner considered by the referee to be dangerous, e.g. attempting to kick the ball while held by the goalkeeper;

2.  charging fairly, i.e. with the shoulder, when the ball is not within playing distance of the

players concerned and they are definitely not trying to play it;

3. when not playing the ball, intentionally obstructing an opponent, i.e. running between the opponent and the ball, or interposing the body so as to form an obstacle to an opponent;

4. charging the goalkeeper except when he

   (a) is holding the ball;

   (b) is obstructing an opponent;

   (c) has passed outside his goal area;

5. when playing as a goalkeeper and within his own penalty area:

   (a) from the moment he takes control of the ball with his hands, he takes more than 4 steps in any direction whilst holding, bouncing or throwing the ball into the air and catching it again, without releasing it into play, or

(b) having released the ball into play before, during or after the 4 steps, he touches it again with his hands, before it has been touched or played by a player of the opposing team either inside or outside of the penalty area, subject to the overriding conditions of 5(c) or

(c) touches the ball with his hands after it has been deliberately kicked to him by a team-mate, or

(d) indulges in tactics, which in the opinion of the referee, are designed to hold up the game and thus waste time and so give an unfair advantage to his own team,

shall be penalised by the award of an indirect free-kick to be taken by the opposing side from the place where the infringement occurred, subject to the overriding conditions imposed in Law XIII.

A player shall be cautioned and shown the yellow card if:

(j) he enters or re-enters the field of play to join or rejoin his team after the game has commenced, or leaves the field of play during the progress of the game (except through accident) without, in either case, first having received a signal from the referee showing him that he may do so.

If the referee stops the game to administer the caution, the game shall be restarted by an indirect free-kick taken by a player of the opposing team from the place where the ball was when the referee stopped the game, subject to the overriding conditions imposed in Law XIII.

If, however, the offending player has committed a more serious offence, he shall be penalised according to that section of the law he infringed.

(k) he persistently infringes the Laws of the Game;

(l)  he shows, by word or action, dissent from any decision given by the referee;

(m)  he is guilty of ungentlemanly conduct.

For any of these last three offences, in addition to the caution, an indirect free-kick shall also be awarded to the opposing side from the place where the offence occurred, subject to the overriding conditions imposed in Law XIII, unless a more serious infringement of the Laws of the Game was committed.

A player shall be sent off the field of play and shown the red card, if, in the opinion of the referee, he:

**RED CARD**

(n)  is guilty of violent conduct;

(o)  is guilty of serious foul play;

(p)  uses foul or abusive language;

(q)  is guilty of a second cautionable of- fence after having received a cau- tion.

If play is stopped by reason of a player being ordered from the field for an offence without a separate breach of the Law having been committed, the game shall be resumed by an indirect free-kick awarded to the opposing side from the place where the infringement occurred, subject to the overriding conditions imposed in Law XIII.

## LAW XII Decisions of the International F.A. Board

(1) If the goalkeeper either intentionally strikes an opponent by throwing the ball vigorously at him or pushes him with the ball while holding it, the referee shall award a penalty-kick, if the offence took place within the penalty-area.

(2) If a player deliberately turns his back to an opponent when he is about to be tackled, he may be charged but not in a dangerous manner.

(3) In case of body contact in the goal-area between an attacking player and the opposing goal-keeper not in possession of the ball, the referee, as sole judge of intention, shall stop the game if, in his opinion, the action of the attacking player was intentional, and award an indirect free-kick.

(4) If a player leans on the shoulders of another player of his own team in order to head the ball, the referee shall stop the game, caution the player for ungentlemanly conduct and award an indirect free-kick to the opposing side.

(5) A player's obligation when joining or rejoining his team after the start of the match to 'report to the referee' must be interpreted as meaning 'to draw the attention of the referee from the touch-line'. The signal from the referee shall be made by a definite gesture which makes the player understand that he may come into the field of play; it is not necessary for the referee to wait until the game is stopped (this does not apply in respect of an infringement of Law IV), but the referee is the sole judge of the moment in which he gives his signal of acknowledgement.

(6) The letter and spirit of Law XII does not oblige the referee to stop a game to administer a caution. He may, if he chooses, apply the advantage. If he does apply the advantage, he shall caution the player when he stops.

(7) If a player covers up the ball without touching it in an endeavour not to have it played by an opponent, he obstructs but does not infringe Law XII para. 3 because he is already in possession of the ball and covers it for tactical reasons whilst the ball remains within playing distance. In fact, he is actually playing the ball and does not commit an infringement; in this case, the player may be charged because he is in fact playing the ball.

(8) If a player intentionally stretches his arms to obstruct an opponent and steps from one side to the other, moving his arms up and down to delay his opponent, forcing him to change course, but does not make "bodily contact" the

referee shall caution the player for ungentlemanly conduct and award an indirect free-kick.

(9) If a player intentionally obstructs the opposing goalkeeper, in an attempt to prevent him from putting the ball into play in accordance with Law XII,5(a), the referee shall award an indirect free kick.

(10) If, after a referee has awarded a free-kick, a player protests violently by using abusive or foul language and is sent off the field, the free-kick should not be taken until the player has left the field.

(11) Any player, whether he is within or outside the field of play, whose conduct is ungentlemanly or violent, whether or not it is directed towards an opponent, a colleague, the referee, a linesman or other person, or who uses foul or abusive language, is guilty of an offence, and shall be dealt with according to the nature of the offence committed.

(12) If, in the opinion of the referee a goalkeeper intentionally lies on the ball longer than is necessary, he shall be penalised for ungentlemanly conduct and

    (a) be cautioned and an indirect free-kick awarded to the opposing team;

    (b) in case of repetition of the offence, be sent off the field.

(13) The offence of spitting at officials and other persons, or similar unseemly behaviour shall be considered as violent conduct within the meaning of section (n) of Law XII.

(14) If, when a referee is about to caution a player, and before he has done so, the player commits another offence which merits a caution, the player shall be sent off the field of play.

(15) If, in the opinion of the referee, a player who is moving toward his opponent's goal with an obvious opportunity to score a goal is intentionally impeded by an opponent, through unlawful means, i.e. an offence punishable by a free kick (or a penalty kick), thus denying the attacking player's team the aforesaid goal-scoring opportunity, the offending player shall be sent off the field of play for serious foul play in accordance with Law XII(n).

(16) If, in the opinion of the referee, a player, other than the goalkeeper within his own penalty area, denies his opponents a goal, or an obvious goal-scoring opportunity, by intentionally handling the ball, he shall be sent off the field of play for serious foul play in accordance with Law XII(n).

(17) The International F.A. Board is of the opinion that a goalkeeper, in the circumstances described in Law XII, 5(a), will be considered to be in control of the ball by touching it with any part of his hands or arms. Possession of the ball would include the goalkeeper intentionally

parrying the ball, but would not include the circumstances where, in the opinion of the referee, the ball rebounds accidentally from the goalkeeper, for example after he has made a save.

(18) Subject to the terms of Law XII, a player may pass the ball to his own goalkeeper using his head or chest or knee, etc. If, however, in the opinion of the referee, a player uses a deliberate trick in order to circumvent article 5(c) of Law XII, the player will be guilty of ungentlemanly conduct and will be punished accordingly under the terms of Law XII; that is to say, the player will be cautioned and shown the yellow card and an indirect free-kick will be awarded to the opposing team from the place where the player committed the offence.

In such circumstances, it is irrelevant whether the goalkeeper subsequently touches the ball with his hands or not. The offence is committed by the player in attempting to circumvent both the text and the spirit of Law XII.

# Free-kick

## LAW XIII **Free-kick**

Free-kicks shall be classified under two headings: "direct" (from which a goal can be scored direct against the offending side), and "indirect" (from which a goal cannot be scored unless the ball has been played or touched by a player other than the kicker before passing through the goal).

When a player is taking a direct or an indirect free-kick inside his own penalty-area, all of the opposing players shall be at least ten yards (9.15 m) from the ball and shall remain outside the penalty-area until the ball has been kicked out of the area. The ball shall be in play immediately after it has travelled the distance of its own circumference and is beyond the penalty-area. The goalkeeper shall not receive the ball into his hands, in order that he may thereafter kick it into play. If the ball is not kicked direct into play, beyond the penalty-area, the kick shall be retaken.

When a player is taking a direct or an indirect free-kick outside his own penalty-area, all of the opposing players shall be at least ten yards from the ball, until it is in play, unless they are standing on their own goal-line, between the goalpost. The ball shall be in play when it has travelled the distance of its own circumference.

If a player of the opposing side encroaches into the penalty-area, or within ten yards of the ball, as the case may be, before a free-kick is taken, the referee shall delay the taking of the kick, until the Law is complied with.

The ball must be stationary when a free-kick is taken, and the kicker shall not play the ball a second time, until it has been touched or played by another player.

Notwithstanding any other reference in these Laws to the point from which a free-kick is to be taken:

1. Any free-kick awarded to the defending team, within its own goal-area, may be taken from any point within the goal-area.

2. Any indirect free-kick awarded to the attacking team within its opponent's goal-area shall be taken

from the part of the goal-area line
which runs parallel to the goal-line,
at the point nearest to where the
offence was committed.

**Punishment:**

If the kicker, after taking the
free-kick, plays the ball a second
time before it has been touched or
played by another player, an
indirect free-kick shall be taken by
a player of the opposing team from
the spot where the infringement
occurred, unless the offence is
committed by a player in his
opponent's goal-area, in which case
the free-kick shall be taken from
any point within the goal-area.

## LAW XIII Decisions of the International F.A. Board

(1) In order to distinguish between a direct and an
indirect free-kick, the referee, when he awards
an indirect free-kick, shall indicate accordingly
by raising an arm above his head. He shall keep
his arm in that position until the kick has been
taken and retain the signal until the ball has
been played or touched by another player or
goes out of play.

(2) Players who do not retire to the proper distance when a free-kick is taken must be cautioned and on any repetition be ordered off. It is particularly requested of referees that attempts to delay the taking of a free-kick by encroaching should be treated as a serious misconduct.

(3) If, when a free-kick is being taken, any of the players dance about or gesticulate in a way calculated to distract their opponents, it shall be deemed ungentlemanly conduct for which the offender(s) shall be cautioned.

# Penalty-kick

# LAW XIV **Penalty-kick**

A penalty-kick shall be taken from the penalty-mark and, when it is being taken, all players with the exception of the player taking the kick, properly identified, and the opposing goalkeeper, shall be within the field of play but outside the penalty-area, and at least 10 yards from the penalty-mark. The opposing goalkeeper must stand (without moving his feet) on his own goal-line, between the goal-posts, until the ball is kicked. The player taking the kick must kick the ball forward; he shall not play the ball a second time until it has been touched or played by another player. The ball shall be deemed in play directly it is kicked i.e. when it has travelled the distance of its circumference. A goal may be scored directly from a penalty-kick. When a penalty-kick is being taken during the normal course of play, or when time has been extended at half-time or full-time to allow a penalty-kick to be taken or retaken, a goal shall not be nullified if, before passing between the posts and under the cross-bar, the ball touches either or both of the goal-posts, or the cross-bars, or the goal-keeper, or any combination of these agencies, providing that no other infringement has occurred.

**Punishment:**

For any infringement of this Law:

(a) by the defending team, the kick shall be retaken if a goal has not resulted.

(b) by the attacking team other than by the player taking the kick, if a goal is scored it shall be disallowed and the kick re-taken.

(c) by the player taking the penalty-kick, committed after the ball is in play, a player of the opposing team shall take an indirect free-kick from the spot where the infringement occurred, subject to the overriding conditions imposed in Law XIII.

## LAW XIV  Decisions of the International F.A. Board

(1) When the referee has awarded a penalty-kick, he shall not signal for it to be taken, until the players have taken up position in accordance with the Law.

(2) (a) If, after the kick has been taken, the ball is stopped in its course towards the goal, by an outside agent, the kick shall be retaken.

    (b) If, after the kick has been taken, the ball rebounds into play, from the goalkeeper, the cross-bar or a goal-post, and is then stopped in its course by an outside agent, the referee shall stop play and restart it by dropping the ball at the place where it came into contact with the outside agent, unless it was within the goal area at that time, in which case it shall be dropped on that part of the goal-area line which runs parallel to the goal-line, at the point nearest to where the ball was when play was stopped.

(3) (a) If, after having given the signal for a penalty-kick to be taken, the referee sees that the goalkeeper is not in his right place on the goal-line, he shall, nevertheless, allow the kick to proceed. It shall be retaken, if a goal is not scored.

    (b) If, after the referee has given the signal for a penalty-kick to be taken, and before the ball has been kicked, the goal-keeper moves his feet, the referee shall, nevertheless, allow the kick to proceed. It shall be retaken, if a goal is not scored.

(c) If, after the referee has given the signal for a penalty-kick to be taken, and before the ball is in play, a player of the defending team encroaches into the penalty-area, or within ten yards of the penalty-mark, the referee shall, nevertheless, allow the kick to proceed. It shall be retaken, if a goal is not scored.

The player concerned shall be cautioned.

(4) (a) If, when a penalty-kick is being taken, the player taking the kick is guilty of ungentlemanly conduct, the kick, if already taken, shall be retaken, if a goal is scored.

The player concerned shall be cautioned.

(b) If, after the referee has given the signal for a penalty-kick to be taken, and before the ball is in play, a colleague of the player taking the kick encroaches into the penalty-area or within ten yards of the penalty-mark, the referee shall, nevertheless, allow the kick to proceed. If a goal is scored, it shall be disallowed, and the kick retaken.

The players concerned shall be cautioned.

(c) If, in the circumstances described in the foregoing paragraph, the ball rebounds into play from the goalkeeper, the cross-bar or a goal-post, and a goal has not been scored, the referee shall stop the game, caution the player and award an indirect free-kick to the opposing team from the place where the infringement occurred, subject to the over-riding conditions imposed in Law XIII.

(5) (a) If, after the referee has given the signal for a penalty-kick to be taken, and before the ball is in play, the goalkeeper moves from his position on the goal-line, or moves his feet, and a colleague of the kicker encroaches into the penalty-area or within 10 yards of the penalty-mark, the kick, if taken, shall be retaken.

The colleague of the kicker shall be cautioned.

(b) If, after the referee has given the signal for a penalty-kick to be taken, and before the ball is in play, a player of each team encroaches into the penalty-area, or within 10 yards of the penalty-mark, the kick, if taken, shall be retaken.

The players concerned shall be cautioned.

(6) When a match is extended, at half-time or full-time, to allow a penalty-kick to be taken or re-taken, the extension shall last until the moment that the penalty-kick has been

completed, i.e. until the referee has decided whether or not a goal is scored, and the game shall terminate immediately after the referee has made his decision.

After the player taking the penalty-kick has put the ball into play, no player other than the defending goalkeeper may play or touch the ball before the kick is completed.

(7) When a penalty-kick is being taken in extended time:

    (a) the provisions of all of the foregoing paragraphs, except paragraphs (2)(b) and (4)(c) shall apply in the usual way, and

    (b) in the circumstances described in paragraphs (2)(b) and (4)(c) the game shall terminate immediately the ball rebounds from the goalkeeper, the cross-bar or the goal-post.

# Throw-in

# LAW XV **Throw-in**

When the whole of the ball passes over a touch-line, either on the ground or in the air, it shall be thrown in from the point where it crossed the line, in any direction, by a player of the team opposite to that of the player who last touched it. The thrower at the moment of delivering the ball must face the field of play and part of each foot shall be either on the touch-line or on the ground outside the touch-line. The thrower shall use both hands and shall deliver the ball from behind and over his head. The ball shall be in play immediately after it enters the field of play, but the thrower shall not again play the ball until it has been touched or played by another player. A goal shall not be scored direct from throw-in.

## Punishment:

(a) If the ball is improperly thrown in the throw-in shall be taken by a player of the opposing team.

(b) If the thrower plays the ball a second time before it has been touched or played by another player, an indirect free-kick shall be taken by a player of the opposing team from the place where the infringement occurred, subject to the overriding conditions imposed in Law XIII.

## LAW XV Decisions of the International F.A. Board

(1) If a player taking a throw-in plays the ball a second time by handling it within the field of play before it has been touched or played by another player, the referee shall award a direct free-kick.

(2) A player taking a throw-in must face the field of play with some part of his body.

(3) If, when a throw-in is being taken, any of the opposing players dance about or gesticulate in a way calculated to distract or impede the thrower, it shall be deemed ungentlemanly conduct, for which the offender(s) shall be cautioned.

(4) A throw-in taken from any position other than the point where the ball passed over the touch-line shall be considered to have been improperly thrown in.

# Goal-kick

## LAW XVI **Goal-kick**

When the whole of the ball passes over the goal-line excluding that portion between the goal-posts, either in the air or on the ground, having last been played by one of the attacking team, it shall be kicked direct into play beyond the penalty-area from any point within the goal-area by a player of the defending team. A goalkeeper shall not receive the ball into his hands from a goal-kick in order that he may thereafter kick it into play. If the ball is not kicked beyond the penalty-area, i.e. direct into play, the kick shall be retaken. The kicker shall not play the ball a second time until it has touched or been played by another player. A goal shall not be scored direct from such a kick. Players of the team opposing that of the player taking the goal-kick shall remain outside the penalty-area until the ball has been kicked out of the penalty-area.

### Punishment:

If a player taking a goal-kick plays the ball a second time after it has passed beyond the penalty-area, but before it has touched or been played by another player, an indirect free-kick shall be awarded to the opposing team, to be taken from the place where the infringement occurred, subject to the overriding conditions imposed in Law XIII.

## LAW XVI **Decisions of the International F.A. Board**

(1) When a goal-kick has been taken and the player who has kicked the ball touches it again before it has left the penalty-area, the kick has not been taken in accordance with the Law and must be retaken.

# Corner-kick

# LAW XVII **Corner-kick**

When the whole of the ball passes over the goal-line, excluding that portion between the goal-posts, either in the air or on the ground, having last been played by one of the defending team, a member of the attacking team shall take a corner-kick, i.e. the whole of the ball shall be placed within the quarter circle at the nearest corner-flag post, which must not be moved, and it shall be kicked from that position. A goal may be scored direct from such a kick. Players of the team opposing that of the player taking the corner-kick shall not approach within 10 yards of the ball until it is in play, i.e. it has travelled the distance of its own circumference, nor shall the kicker play the ball a second time until it has been touched or played by another player.

## Punishment:

(a) If the player who takes the kick plays the ball a second time before it has been touched or played by another player, the referee shall award an indirect free-kick to the opposing team, to be taken from the place where the infringement occurred, subject to the overriding conditions imposed in Law XIII.

**(b)** For any other infringement the kick shall be retaken.

# Appendix

# Additional Instructions Regarding the Laws of the Game

The following decisions and instructions to referees conform with the Laws of the Game and the decisions of the International F.A. Board. They are therefore regarded as authoritative and quoted as such.

### 1. Serious foul play and violent conduct

Football being a tough, combative sport—where the contest to gain possession of the ball should nonetheless be fair and gentlemanly — any such moves, even when really vigorous, must be allowed by the referee.

Serious foul play and violent conduct are, however, strictly forbidden and the referee must react to them by stringently applying the Laws of the Game.

These two offences can be defined as follows:

(a) it is a serious foul when a player infringes the Laws of the Game and uses intentional violence when challenging for the ball against an opponent.

(b) it is violent conduct when a player is guilty of aggression towards an opponent even when they are not challenging for the ball. The ball can be in or out of play. If the ball is in play he shall be sanctioned with a direct free kick in favour of the team of the player who was attacked, from the place where the offence was committed, or with a penalty kick if it took place within the penalty area. If the ball is out of play, the game shall be resumed at the stage where it was interrupted prior to the offence (throw-in, free kick, etc.).

Moreover, if a player attacks one of his teammates, the referee, a linesman, a spectator, etc., this shall also be considered violent conduct. As mentioned above, this offence can arise when the ball is in or out of play. If the ball is in play, the player shall be sanctioned with an indirect free kick against his team from the spot where the violent conduct occurred or with a dropped ball taken at the place where the ball was situated at the time of the offence, if this occurred beyond the boundaries of the field of play. If the ball is out of play the game shall be resumed at the stage where it was interrupted prior to the offence (throw-in, free kick, etc.).

## 2. Tackling

(a) A sliding tackle with one or both legs is permissible if, in the opinion of the referee, it is not dangerous. If, however, the player making the tackle, instead of making contact with the ball, trips his opponent, the referee shall award a direct free kick to the opposing team and shall caution the offending player.

(b) A tackle from behind which is violent with little or no attempt to play the ball is prohibited and will

be punished by a direct free kick
and an ordering off.

### 3. Offences against goalkeepers

It is an offence is a player:

(a) jumps at a goalkeeper under the
pretext of heading the ball;

(b) dodges about in front of a
goalkeeper in order to prevent him
from releasing the all;

(c) who is standing in front of a
goalkeeper when a corner kick is
being taken, takes advantage of his
position to obstruct the goalkeeper
before the kick is taken and before
the ball is in play;

(d) attempts to kick the ball when the
goalkeeper is in the process of
releasing it.

### 4. Obstruction

A player who has the ball under control
within playing distance (i.e., the
distance at which the player is covering
the ball for tactical reasons in order to
avoid its being played by an opponent,
without using his arms) is not guilty of
obstruction.

Any player who intentionally obstructs an opponent by crossing directly in front of him or running between him and the ball or intervening so as to form an obstacle with the aim of delaying his advance, must be sanctioned with an indirect free kick in favour of the opposing team.

However, any player who intentionally impedes the progress of an opponent by physical contact, whether using his hand, arm, leg, or any other part of his body, shall be penalized by the award of a direct free kick to the opposing team, or by a penalty kick, if the offence was committed within his penalty area.

## 5. Scissors or bicycle kick

Such a kick is permissible, provided that in the opinion of the referee itis not dangerous to an opponent.

## 6. Jumping at an opponent

A player who jumps at an opponent under the pretext of heading the ball shall be penalised by the award of a direct free kick to the opposing team.

## 7. Prohibited use of body

A player who holds off an opponent using his hand, arm, leg or body, is guilty of an infringement of Law XII and shall be punished by the award of a direct free kick to the opposing team. Holding or hindering an opponent when the ball is out of play in order to prevent him from running into position is an offence (disciplinary punishment).

## 8. Caution for handling the ball or holding an opponent

Whilst it is not usual for a player to be cautioned for handling the ball or holding an opponent, there are exceptional circumstances in which, in addition to imposing the customary punishment, the referee must caution a player for ungentlemanly conduct in these offences:

(a) when a player, in order to prevent an opponent from gaining possession of the ball, and because he is unable to play it in any other way, stops it with one, or both hands, punches it or catches it, or

(b) when a player holds an opponent in order to prevent him from gaining possession of the ball.

(c) when an attacking player attempts to score a goal by illegal use of the hand. The foregoing is subject to the provisions contained in decision 16 of Law XII of the International F.A. Board (obvious goal or goal-scoring opportunity denied = ordering offence).

### 9. Free Kicks

(a) The referee shall indicate the award of an indirect free kick by raising an arm above his head. He shall keep his arm in that position until the kick has been taken and the ball has been played or touched by player or goes out of play.

(b) Any player who, for any reason, deliberately plays a free kick being taken by the opposing team shall be cautioned (yellow card). For repetition of this offence he shall be sent off (red card).

(c) Any player who prematurely rushes forward from the defensive wall,

---

formed at least 10 yards (9.15 m)
from the ball, before the ball has
been kicked, shall be cautioned. In
the event of repetition of this
offence, he shall be sent off.

While the Law states that all opposing
players should retire to a distance of at
least 10 yards (9.15m) from the ball,
the referee has discretionary power to
disregard this requirement to enable a
free kick to be taken quickly.

### 10. Penalty kick

(a) **Conduct during a penalty kick**
During a penalty kick, the
goalkeeper shall stand on the
goal-line without moving his feet.
Apart from the goalkeeper and the
player taking the kick, all the
players shall take up position
outside the penalty area at least 10
yards (9.15m) away from the
penalty mark and stay there until
the kick has been taken.
Any breach of these conditions
shall be dealt with in accordance
with Law XIV.

(b) Penalty kick at the end of the first
half or at the end of the match

If play is prolonged before half-time or at the end of the match to allow for a penalty kick to be taken or for one to be retaken, a goal shall not be disallowed if, before passing the goalposts under the crossbar, the ball touches one of the two goalposts or the crossbar or goalkeeper, or a combination of these, providing no infringement has been committed.

## 11. Player in offside position

(a) It is not an offence in itself to be in an offside position.

(b) A player shall be penalised for being offside, if, at the moment the ball touches, or is played by, one of his team, he is, in the opinion of the referee involved in the active play by

1. interfering with play or with an opponent, or

2. seeking to gain an advantage by being in that position.

(c) A player shall not be declared offside by the referee

1. merely because of his being in an offside position, or

2. if he receives the ball directly from a goal-kick, a corner kick or a throw-in.

A linesman should not signal merely because a player is in an offside position.

## 12. Goalkeepers

The following principles shall apply: A goalkeeper who is within his own penalty area:

(a) from the moment he takes control of the ball with his hands, takes more than 4 steps in any direction whilst holding, bouncing or throwing the bal in the air and catching it again, without releasing it into play, or, having released the ball into play before, during or after the 4 steps, he touches it again with his hands, before it has been touched or played by another player of the same team outside of the penalty area, or by a player of the opposing team either inside or outside of the penalty area subject to the overriding conditions of Law XII, 5(c), or

(b) indulges in tactics which, in the opinion of the referee, are designed merely to hold up the game and thus waste time and so give an unfair advantage to his own team, shall be penalised by the award of an indirect free kick to be taken by the opposing team from the place where the infringement occurred. Furthermore, attention must be paid to the contents of decision 17 of Law XII of the International F.A. Board.

### 13. Persistent Infringements

Any player who persistently infringes the Laws of the Game shall be cautioned.

### 14. Player sent off after receiving two cautions

If a player is sent off for committing a second cautionable offence, the referee shall first show the yellow card followed immediately by the red card (so that it is obvious that the player is being sent off for the second cautionable offence and not for an offence requiring immediate expulsion).

### 15. **Substitution**

A player who is going to be replaced may not leave the field of play without the referee's permission and then only when the ball is out of play.
The substitute may then enter the field at the halfway line only.

### 16. **Injury of a player**

Team officials are permitted to enter the field of play with the referee's permission solely for the purpose of assessing an injury—not to treat it—and to arrange for the player's removal.

### 17. **Attitude toward referees**

Any player who protests at a referee's decision shall be cautioned.
Any player who assaults or insults a referee shall be sent off.
The captain of a team, although reponsible for his team's behavior, has no special rights.

### 18. **Throw-in**

A throw-in may not be taken from a distance of more than one metre outside the touch-line. Players are forbidden from standing directly in front of the footballer who is taking the throw-in so as to harass him.

### 19. Wasting time

Any player who wastes time shall be cautioned for ungentlemanly conduct. Wasting time occurs whenever:

(a) a player:
—feigns injury;
—takes a free kick from a wrong position with the sole intention of forcing the referee to demand a retake;
—appears to prepare for a throw-in but suddenly leaves it to one of his team to throw in;
—kicks the ball away or carries it away with the hands after the referee has stopped play for any reason;
—stands in front of the ball when a free kick has been awarded to the opposing team in order to give his team time to organise the defensive wall;
—excessively delays taking a throw-in or a free kick;
—delays leaving the field when being substituted.

**(b)** a goalkeeper:
—employs all manner of tactics with the sole intention of gaining time for his team (keeping the ball longer than necessary, waiting too long before passing it into play, etc.)

## 20. Celebration of goal

After a goal has been scored, the player who has scored it is allowed to share his joy with his team-mates. However, the referee must not allow them to spend an inordinate amount of time in their opponents' half of the field. Neither will he tolerate players dashing past the billboards or climbing up the crowd barriers. In either of these last two cases, he will caution the offending player for ungentlemanly conduct.

## 21. Liquid refreshments during the match

Players shall be entitled to take liquid refreshments during a stoppage in the match but only on the touchline. It is forbidden to throw plastic water bags or any other water containers onto the field.

## 22. Inspection of studs

The referee, assisted by his linesmen, shall inspect the players' studs in the corridor leading from the dressing rooms to the fields, as they are about to go on the field for the start of the match.

## 23. Players' outfits

(a) The referee shall ensure that each player wears his clothes properly and check that they conform with the requirements of Law IV. Players shall be made aware that their jersey remains tucked inside their shorts and that their socks remain pulled up. The referee shall also make sure that each player is wearing shinguards and that none of them is wearing potentially dangerous objects (such as watches, metal bracelets, etc.).

(b) Players are permitted to wear visible undergarments such as thermopants. They must, however, be the same color as the shorts of the team of the player wearing them and not extend beyond the top of the knee. If a team wears multicoloured shorts, the undergarment must be the same colour as the predominant colour.

# Instructions regarding the Taking of Kicks from the Penalty-mark

(In knock-out competitions to decide the winner)

**Conditions under which kicks from the penalty-mark shall be taken to determine which of the two teams in a drawn match, in a knock-out competition, shall be declared the winner.**

(To replace drawing lots)

The International Board at its meeting on 27 June 1970 accepted a proposal by the Fédération Internationale de Football Association that the practice of drawing lots to determine which of two teams in a drawn match should proceed to a later stage of a knock-out competition or receive the trophy (if any) be discontinued and be replaced by the taking of kicks from the penalty-mark which shall not be considered part of the match, subject to the following conditions:

1. The referee shall choose the goal at which all of the kicks shall be taken.

2. He shall toss a coin, and the team whose captain wins the toss shall take the first kick.

3. The referee shall note each player as he takes a kick from the penalty-mark.

4.(a) Subject to the terms of the following paragraphs (c) and (d) both teams shall take five kicks.

  (b) The kicks shall be taken alternately.

  (c) If, before both teams have taken five kicks, one has scored more goals than the other could, even if it were to complete its five kicks, the taking of kicks shall cease.

  (d) If, after both teams have taken five kicks, both have scored the same number of goals or have not scored any goals, the taking of kicks shall continue, in the same order, until such time as both have taken an equal number of kicks (not necessarily five more kicks) and one has scored a goal more than the other.

5. The team which scores the greater number of goals, whether the number of kicks taken is in accordance with the terms of the foregoing paragraph 4(a), 4(c), 4(d) shall qualify for the next round of the competition, or shall be declared winner of the competition, as the case may be.

6.(a) With the exception referred to in the following paragraph (b) only the players who are on the field of play at the end of the match, which shall mean at the end of extra time in so far as a match in which extra time is authorised is concerned, and any who, having left the field temporarily with or without the referee's permission, are not on the field of play at that time, shall take part in the taking of the kicks.

(b) Provided that his team has not already made use of the maximum number of substitutes permitted by the rules of the competition under which the match was played, a goalkeeper who sustains an injury during the taking of the kicks and who, because of the injury, is unable to continue as goalkeeper, may be replaced by a substitute.

7. Each kick shall be taken by a different player, and not until all eligible players of any team, including the goalkeeper or the named substitute by whom he was replaced under the terms of paragraph 6 as the case may be, have each taken a kick, may a player of the same team take a second kick.

8. Subject to the terms of paragraph 6, any player who is eligible may change places with his goalkeeper at any time during the taking of the kicks.

9.(a) Other than the player taking a kick from the penalty-mark, and the two goalkeepers, all players shall remain within the centre circle whilst the taking of kicks is in progress.

(b) The goalkeeper who is a colleague of the kicker, shall take up position within the field of play, outside the penalty area at which the kicks are being taken behind the line which runs parallel with the goal-line, and at least 10 yards from the penalty-mark.

(c) The goalkeeper is reminded that he must remain on the goal-line between the posts until the ball is kicked into play.

10. Unless stated to the contrary in the foregoing paragraphs 1 to 9, the Laws of the Game, and the International Board Decisions relating thereto, shall, in so far as they can, apply at the taking of the kicks.

*N.B.: In the event of light failing before the end of the taking of kicks from the penalty-mark, the result shall be decided by the toss of a coin or drawing lots.*

# Taking of Kicks from the Penalty-mark
# Checklist for Referees

1. Decide at which end the kicks will be taken. This can be an important decision if the supporters of one team are behind one goal and those of the other team are at the opposite goal.

2. The team which wins the toss must take the first kick.

3. Before the kicks begin, ensure that all team officials, etc., have left the field and that only the players are left.

4. Make sure all players, apart from the kicker and the two goalkeepers are inside the centre circle.

5. Make sure the goalkeeper of the kicker's team stands outside the penalty area, in the position shown in the diagram.

6. The Laws of the Game, particularly Law XIV "The Penalty Kick", apply except where modified by the instructions for the taking of kicks

from the penalty-mark. Be particularly vigilant therefore for instances of gamesmanship or for infringements by the goalkeeper, e.g. moving before the ball is kicked.

7. Keep a careful record of the kicks taken.

8. Where you have the assistance of neutral linesmen some of those duties may be taken by them, e.g. a linesman at the centre circle would organise players coming to take the kick while the other linesman would assist by indicating whether or not the ball has crossed the goal-line.

9. It is very important that the referee organises the taking of kicks from the penalty-mark correctly. Make sure you fully understand the instructions.

10. The taking of kicks from the penalty-mark never forms part of an actual match. It is only a method of deciding a winner.

11. If, at the taking of kicks from the penalty-mark, the light fails badly and the kicks therefore cannot be completed, the result shall be decided by tossing a coin or drawing lots.

12. An injured player may be excused from the taking of kicks from the penalty-mark.

13. It is the responsibility of each team to select the players who will take the kicks from the penalty-mark. The referee's only duty is to ensure that they are taken correctly.

14. When all the players in a team have taken a kick from the penalty-mark, it is not necessary that they follow the same order in taking their second kick as they had for the first series of kicks.

15. If a player who has already been cautioned commits a second cautionable offence at the taking of kicks from the penalty-mark, he shall be sent off.

16. When the lights fail at a stadium after extra time but before the taking of kicks from the penalty-mark, if they cannot be repaired in a reasonable time, the referee shall decide the match by tossing a coin or drawing lots.

17. A substitute who has not taken part in the match, including extra time where it is played, may not take part in kicks

from the penalty-mark, except to replace an injured goalkeeper.

18. After each team has taken 10 kicks from the penalty-mark, a team which has had a player sent off may use a player who has already taken a kick for the 11th kick.

19. If at the end of the match some players leave the field of play and fail to return for the taking of kicks from the penalty-mark, and are not injured, the referee shall not allow the kicks to be taken and shall report the matter to the responsible authorities.

20. If, at the taking of kicks from the penalty-mark, or when extended time is being allowed for a penalty-kick to be taken in normal playing time, the ball strikes the goalpost or crossbar, strikes the goalkeeper and enters the goal, a goal shall be awarded.

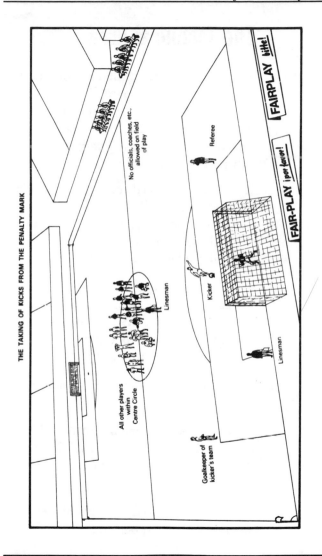

THE TAKING OF KICKS FROM THE PENALTY MARK

No officials, coaches, etc., allowed on field of play

Referee

Linesman

All other players within Centre Circle

Kicker

Linesman

Goalkeeper of kicker's team

FAIRPLAY bitte!

FAIR-PLAY ¡por favor!

# The Technical Area

The technical area as defined in Law V, International F.A. Board Decision no. 13, relates particularly to matches played in stadia with a designated seated area for technical staff and substitutes as shown below.

It is recognized that technical areas may vary between stadia, for example, in size or location, but notwithstanding, the following notes are issued for general guidance.

1. The technical area shall be considered as extending 1 metre on either side of the designated seated area and shall extend forward up to a distance of 1 metre away from the touchline.

2. Markings are not required to define this area.

3. The number of persons permitted to occupy the technical area shall be defined by the rules of the competition.

4. The occupants of the technical area shall be identified before the

commencement of the match in accordance with the rules of the competition.

5. Only one person has the authority to convey tactical instructions and he must return to his position immediately after giving these instructions.

6. The coach and other officials must remain within the confines of the technical area except in special circumstances, for example, a physio or doctor entering the field of play with the referee's permission to treat an injured player.

7. The coach and other occupants of the technical area must conduct themselves, at all times, in a responsible manner.

# The Role of the Fourth Official

1. He may be appointed under the rules of a competition and shall officiate in the event of any of the three match officials being unable to continue.

2. The organiser, prior to the start of the competition, shall state clearly whether, in the event of any referee being unable to continue, the fourth official would take over as the match referee or whether the senior linesman would take over as referee with the fourth official becoming a linesman.

3. The fourth official shall assist with any administrative duties before, during and after the match as required by the referee.

4. He shall be responsible for assisting with substitution procedures during the match.

5. He shall control the replacement footballs where required. If during a match the match ball has to be replaced he shall, on the instructions of

the referee, provide another ball thus keeping the time delay to a minimum.

6. He shall have the authority to check the equipment of substitutes prior to their entering the field of play. In the event of their equipment not being within the Laws of the Game he shall inform the linesman who shall then inform the referee.

7. While the fourth official has no status within the Laws of the Game, his duties will be to assist the referee at all times.

# Diagrams Illustrating Points in Connections with OFF-SIDE

The players marked ⊗ are attacking the goal and those marked ◯ are defending

Direction of movement of ball:
– – – – – – – – ►

**Diagram 1 – OFF-SIDE**

Direction of movement of player:
—————————►

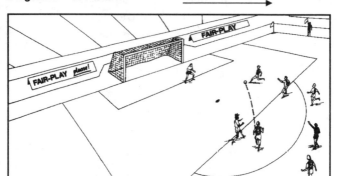

**Clear pass to one of the same side**

**A** is in possession of the ball, and having **Y** in front passes to **B**.

**B** is off-side because he is in front of **A** and there are not at least two opponents between him and the goal-line when the ball is passed by **A**.

If **B** waits for **Z** to fall back before he shoots, this will not put him on-side, because it does not alter his position with relation to **A** at the moment the ball was passed by **A**.

## Diagram 2 – NOT OFF-SIDE

### Clear pass to one of the same side (continued)

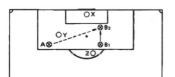

**A** is in possession of the ball, and having **Y** in front passes across the field. **B** runs from position **1** to position **2**.
**B** is not off-side because at the moment the ball was passed by **A** he was not in front of the ball, and had at least two opponents between him and the goal-line.

**Diagram 3 – OFF-SIDE**

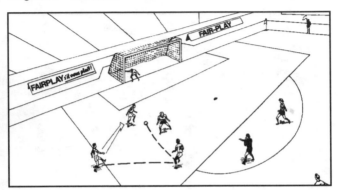

**Clear pass to one of the same side (continued)**

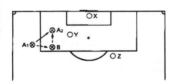

A and B make a passing run up the wing. A passes the ball to B who cannot shoot because he has Y in front. A then runs from position 1 to position 2 and B then passes the ball to him.

A is off-side because he is in front of the ball and there are not at least two opponents between him and the goal-line when the ball was played by B.

**Diagram 4 – NOT OFF-SIDE**

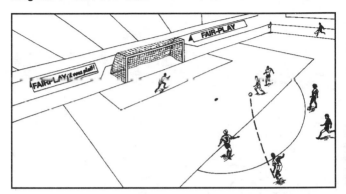

**Clear pass to one of the same side (continued)**

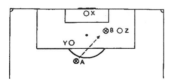

A is in possession of the ball, and having **Y** in front passes to **B**.

**B** is not off-side because he is not nearer to his opponents' goal-line than at least two opponents when the ball is passed by **A**.

## Diagram 5 – NOT OFF-SIDE

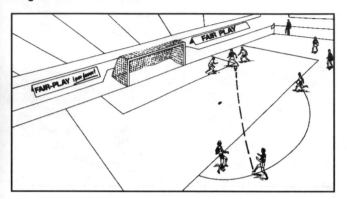

**Clear pass to one of the same side (continued)**

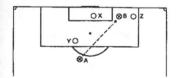

A is in possession of the ball, and having Y in front passes to B.

B is not off-side because he is level with X and Z when the ball is passed by A and is therefore not nearer his opponents' goal-line than at least two of his opponents.

## Diagram 6 – OFF-SIDE

### Running back for the ball

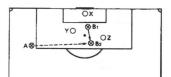

A centres the ball. B runs back from position 1 to position 2, and then dribbles between Y and Z and scores.

B is off-side because he is in front of the ball and there were not at least two opponents between him and the goal-line at the moment the ball was played by A.

**Diagram 7 – OFF-SIDE**

**Running back for the ball (continued)**

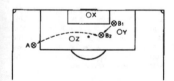

**A** makes a high shot at goal, and the wind and screw carry the ball back. **B** runs from position **1** to position **2** and scores.
**B** is off-side because he is in front of the ball and there were not at least two opponents between him and the goal-line at the moment the ball was played by **A**.

**Diagram 8 – OFF-SIDE**

**Shot at goal returned by goalkeeper (X)**

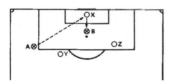

**A** shoots at goal. The ball is played by **X** and **B** obtains possession.

**B** is off-side because he was in front of **A** when the ball was played by **A** and **B** did not have at least two opponents between him and the goal-line.

## Diagram 9 – OFF-SIDE

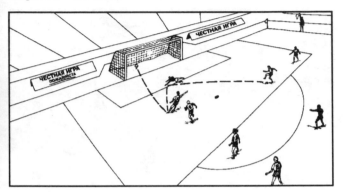

### Shot at goal returned by goalkeeper (continued)

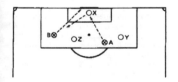

A shoots at goal. The ball is played out by X but B obtains possession and scores. The goal should be disallowed if the referee considers that B, who is in an off-side position when A shoots, is interfering with play.

## Diagram 10 – OFF-SIDE

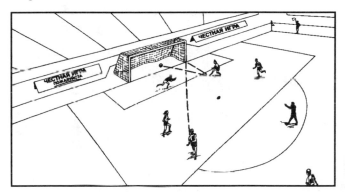

### Ball rebounding from goal-posts or cross-bar

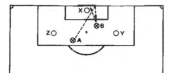

A shoots for goal and the ball rebounds from the goal-post into play. B secures the ball and scores.

B is off-side because the ball is last played by A, a player of his own side, and when A played it B was in front of the ball and did not have at least two opponents between him and the goal-line.

## Diagram 11 – OFF-SIDE

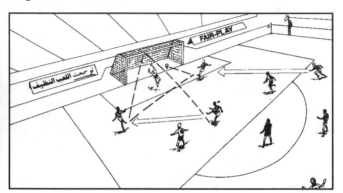

### Ball rebounding from goal-posts or cross-bar (continued)

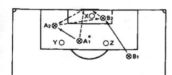

**A** shoots for goal and the ball rebounds from the cross-bar into play. **A** follows up from position **1** to position **2**, and then passes to **B** who has run up on the other side.

**B** is off-side because the ball is last played by **A**, a player of his own side, and when **A** played it **B** was in front of the ball and did not have at least two opponents between him and the goal-line. If **A** kicks the ball directly into the goal from his new position instead of passing to **B**, the referee should award a goal if he considers that **B** in his new position at **B2** is neither interfering with play or an opponent or seeking to gain an advantage.

## Diagram 12 – OFF-SIDE

### Ball touching an opponent

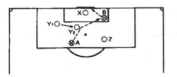

A shoots at goal. Y runs from position **1** to position **2** to intercept the ball, but it glances off his foot to **B** who scores.

**B** is off-side as he was in an off-side position at the moment the ball was played by one of his own team and interfering with play notwithstanding that the ball was deflected by **Y**.

## Diagram 13 – OFF-SIDE

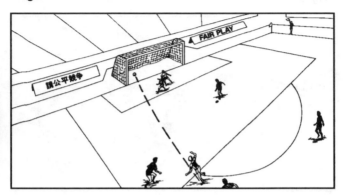

### Obstructing the goalkeeper

**A** shoots for goal and scores. **B**, however, obstructs **X** so that he cannot get at the ball.

The goal must be disallowed, because **B** is in an off-side position and may not touch the ball himself, nor in any way whatever interfere with an opponent.

## Diagram 14 – OFF-SIDE

### Obstructing the goalkeeper (continued)

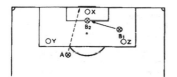

**A** shoots for goal. **B** runs in while the ball is in transit and prevents **X** playing it properly.

**B** is off-side because he is in front of **A** and there are not at least two opponents between him and the goal-line when **A** plays the ball. When in this position **B** may not touch the ball himself, nor in any way whatever interfere with an opponent.

**Diagram 15 – OFF-SIDE**

**Obstructing an opponent other than the goalkeeper**

**A** shoots for goal. **B** prevents **Z** running in to intercept the ball.

**B** is off-side because he is in front of **A** and there are not at least two opponents between him and the goal-line when **A** plays the ball. When in this position, **B** may not touch the ball himself nor in any way whatever interfere with an opponent.

**Diagram 16 – OFF-SIDE**

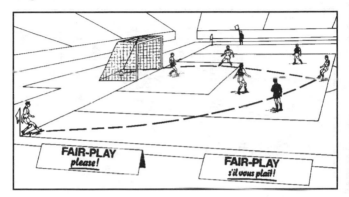

### After a corner-kick

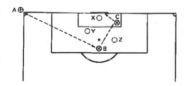

**A** takes a corner-kick and the ball goes to **B**. **B** shoots for goal and as the ball is passing through, **C** touches it.

**C** is off-side because after the corner-kick has been taken the ball is last played by **B**, a player of his own side, and when **B** played it **C** was in front of the ball and there were not at least two opponents between him and the goal-line.

**Diagram 17 – NOT OFF-SIDE**

**After a corner-kick (continued)**

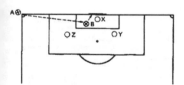

**A** takes a corner-kick and the ball goes to **B**, who scores.

**B** has only one opponent between him and the goal-line, but he is not off-side because a player cannot be off-side from a corner-kick.

**Diagram 18 – NOT OFF-SIDE**

### After a corner-kick (continued)

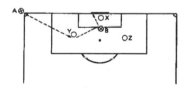

**A** takes a corner-kick and the ball glances off **Y** and goes to **B**, who scores.
The goal should be allowed as **B** was not off-side when the ball was last played by a member of his own team.

## Diagram 19 – OFF-SIDE

**After a throw-in from the touch-line**

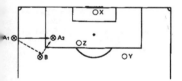

**A** throws to **B** and then runs from the touch-line to position **A2**. **B** passes the ball to **A** in position **2**.

**A** is off-side because he is in front of the ball and there are not at least two opponents between him and the goal-line when the ball is passed forward to him by **B**.

## Diagram 20 – NOT OFF-SIDE

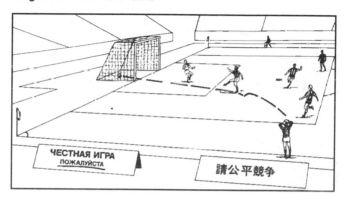

**After a throw-in from the touch-line (continued)**

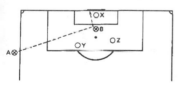

**A** throws the ball to **B**.
Although **B** is in front of the ball and there are not at least two opponents between him and the goal-line, he is not off-side because a player cannot be off-side from a throw-in.

**Diagram 21 – OFF-SIDE**

### A player cannot put himself on-side by running back into his own half of the field of play

If **A** is in his opponents' half of the field of play and is off side in that position when **B** last played the ball, he cannot put himself on-side by moving back into his own half of the field of play.

## Diagram 22 – NOT OFF-SIDE

**A player within his own half of the field of play is not off-side
when he enters his opponents' half of the field of play**

If **A** is in his own half of the field of play he is on-side, although he is in front of the ball and there are not at least two opponents nearer their own goal-line when **B** last played the ball. **A** is therefore not off-side when he enters his opponents' half of the field of play.

---

# Co-operation between the referee and linesmen

In the Laws of the Game set out in the foregoing pages there are no instructions as to the relative positioning of the referee and linesmen during a game. There are, however, instructions in Laws V and VI with regard to the powers and duties of the referee and linesmen which, rightly interpreted, imply co-operation. Law VI stipulates that two linesmen shall be appointed, whose duty (subject to the decision of the referee) shall be to:

(a) signal when the ball is out of play;

(b) signal when the ball has crossed the goal-line and whether a corner-kick or a goal-kick is to be awarded;

(c) signal which side is entitled to the throw in;

(d) assist the referee in conducting the game in accordance with the Laws.

The assistance referred to in (d) consists of:

1. signalling when the whole of the ball is out of play;

2. indicating which side is entitled to the corner-kick, the goal-kick, or the throw-in;

3. calling the attention of the referee to rough play or ungentlemanly conduct;

4. indicating to the referee when a substitution is desired;

5. giving an opinion on any point on which the referee may consult him.

### Neutral linesmen

The assistance referred to above is best given by neutral linesmen. A limitation is placed upon club linesmen because points 2., 3. and 4. are not usually referred to linesmen who are not neutral. Neutral linesmen must act as assistant referees. In this case, the referee must adopt the appropriate attitude, because in effect there are three officials supervising play; the referee as principal official and the linesmen to assist him to control the game in a proper manner.

## Club linesmen

To acquire the most effective co-operation from club linesmen, the following procedure shall be adopted:

1. Both club linesmen shall report to the referee before the start of the match for instructions. He shall inform them that, regardless of their personal opinion, his decision is final and must not be questioned.

2. Their work as club linesmen is to signal when the ball is entirely over the touch-line and to indicate which side is entitled to the throw-in, subject always to the decision of the referee.

Keeping in mind their distinct duties as outlined above, the referee shall decide beforehand exactly what he requires of the club linesmen and as head of the trio, tell them clearly how they can best assist him. The three officials must therefore confer before the match and the referee's instructions must be specific in order to avoid confusion. The linesmen must, for their part, fully appreciate the referee's supreme authority and accept his rulings without question should there be any difference of opinion amongst them. They must be supportive and never contradict his decisions.

The referee shall use the diagonal system of control if his linesmen are neutral. If they are not, neutral, he shall inform them which method he intends to use. He shall co-operate with his linesmen on the following matters and tell them:

(a) the time by his watch;

(b) the side of the field which each linesman shall take in each half of the match;

(c) their duties prior to the start of the game, such as checking the appurtenances on the field;

(d) who shall be the senior linesman if need be;

(e) their positioning during corner-kicks;

(f) the sign denoting that he has noticed his linesman's signal but has overruled it;

(g) which detail in the throw-in shall be observed by the linesman and which by the referee. Some referees ask their linesmen to watch out for foot faults while they themselves concentrate on hand faults.

Referees must not necessarily keep to one diagonal of the field of play. If the state of the ground or the weather demands a switch to the opposite diagonal, the referee shall indicate his intention to make such a change-over to the linesmen, who shall immediately move to the other half of their line. One advantage of such a change in diagonal is that the surface of the ground next to the touch-line will be less worn out because the whole length of the field will be utilised.

Other methods of co-operation may be used as long as all three officials are aware of them.

The following diagrams illustrate the diagonal system of control and, if studied and implemented, will lead to uniform methods of control.

# Signals by the Referee and Linesmen

The signals illustrated in this memorandum have been approved by the International F.A. Board for use by registered referees of affiliated National Associations.

Illustrations concerning signals by the referee are shown on pages 166-173. They are simple, universally in use, and well understood.

While it is not the duty of the referee to explain or mime any offence that has caused him to give a particular decision, there are times when a simple gesture or word of guidance can aid communication and assist toward greater understanding, and gaining more respect, to the mutual benefit of referee and players. Improving communication should be encouraged, but the exaggerated miming of offences can be undignified and confusing and should not be used.

An indication by the referee of the point where a throw-in should be

taken may well help prevent a player
from taking a throw-in improperly.
A call of "Play on, advantage" confirms
to a player that the referee has not
simply missed a foul, but has chosen to
apply advantage. Even an indication
that the ball was minutely deflected by
its touching another player on its path
across a touch-line might be helpful
too in generating a greater
understanding between referee and
players. A better understanding will
lead to more harmonious relationships.

All signals given by the referee should
be simple, clear and instinctive. They
should be designed to control the game
efficiently and to ensure continuous
play as far as possible; they are
intended essentially to indicate what
the next action in the game should
be, not principally to justify that
action.

An arm pointing to indicate a
corner-kick, goal-kick or foul, and the
direction in which it is to be taken, will
normally be sufficient. The raised arm
to indicate that a free-kick is indirect is
clearly understood, but if a player
queries politely whether the award is a
direct free-kick or an indirect free kick,

a helpful word from the referee, in addition to the regular signal, will lead to a better understanding in the future.

The duties of the referee and linesmen are set out briefly but clearly in the Laws of the Game, Laws V and VI.

There is further exposition of cooperation between the referee and linesmen in the memorandum explaining the universally adopted system of "diagonal control".

The proper use of the whistle, voice and hand signals by the referee and the flags by the linesmen should all assist understanding through clear communication.

## Co-operation between linesmen and referee

When play has been stopped the linesman shall assist the referee by signalling the following manner for the following incidents:

1. **Off-side**. The linesman shall lower his flag at full arm's length to the positions illustrated, and point across the field of play to indicate the spot from which the kick shall

be taken. The only exception would be where the referee has decided to position himself to judge off-side when play develops from a corner-kick, penalty-kick or free-kick close to goal.

2. **Throw-in.** When the ball goes out of play over the touch-line on his side of the field, the linesman shall indicate the direction of the throw. He shall also signal if the thrower's feet, at the moment of release of the ball, are incorrectly placed.

3. **Corner-and goal-kicks.** When the whole of the ball goes out of play over the goal-line the linesman shall indicate whether a corner-kick or goal-kick shall be given.

4. **Goal.** When the referee indicated that a goal has been scored the linesman shall return quickly to his position towards the half-way line.

5. **Substitution.** When a substitution is to be made, the linesman nearest to the point of substitution shall attract the attention of the referee by raising his flag as shown in the

illustration included in "Signals by the Linesmen" on pages 181-182 .

**Law XII.** If the linesman senses that the referee has not seen an infringement, he shall raise his flag high. If the referee stops play, the linesman shall indicate the direction of the free-kick (direct or indirect), otherwise he shall lower his flag.

(Illustrations concerning signals by the linesman see pages 175-182.)

**Play On – Advantage**

Where the referee sees an offence but uses the "advantage", he shall indicate that play shall continue.

### Penalty-kick

The referee clearly indicates the penalty-mark, but there is no need to run towards it.

### Indirect free-kick

This signal shall be maintained until the kick has been taken and retained until the ball has been played or touched by another player or goes out of play.

### Direct free-kick

The hand and arm clearly indicate the direction.

**Goal-kick**

**Goal-kick**

## Corner-kick

## Caution or expulsion

With the card system, the card shall be shown in the manner illustrated. The player's identity must be recorded at the same time.

**Off-side**

Flag held upright to indicate off-side.

### Off-side

When the referee stops play, the linesman indicates the position on the far
side of the field.

## Off-side

Position near the centre of the field.

**Off-side**

Position on the near side of the field.

**Throw-in**

### Corner-kick

The linesman may first need to signal that the ball has gone out of play if there is any doubt. He should also look at the referee in case he has already made his own decision, which may be different from the linesman's.

**Goal-kick**

### Substitution

Back view of the linesman signalling to the referee for a substitution to be made.

## Substitution

Front view of the linesman signalling to
the referee when a substitute is waiting
at the lines.